A DIALOGUE

ON

PERSONAL IDENTITY

AND

IMMORTALITY

A DIALOGUE

ON

PERSONAL IDENTITY

AND

IMMORTALITY

John Perry

HACKETT PUBLISHING COMPANY
Indianapolis

Interior design by James N. Rogers

Copyright © 1978 by John Perry

10 09 08 07 06   14 15 16 17 18

For further information, address
Hackett Publishing Company, Inc.
Box 44937
Indianapolis, Indiana 46244-0937

Printed in the United States of America

ISBN-13: 987-0-915144-91-4 (cloth)
ISBN-10: 0-915144-91-3 (cloth)
ISBN-13: 978-0-915144-53-2 (pbk.)
ISBN-10: 0-915144-53-0 (pbk.)

Library of Congress Catalog Card Number 78-52943

AUTHOR'S NOTE

I wrote this paper while a Guggenheim Fellow and on sabbatical leave from Stanford University. I would like to thank both institutions for their support.

My aim has not been to explain and defend my own views on personal identity, but to introduce and develop positions and arguments that have emerged in the literature on that topic.

AUTHORS' NOTE

A DIALOGUE on PERSONAL IDENTITY and IMMORTALITY

> This _is a record of conversations of Gretchen
> Weirob, a teacher of philosophy at a small mid-
> western college, and two of her friends. The
> conversations took place in her hospital room on
> the three nights before she died from injuries
> sustained in a motorcycle accident. Sam Miller is
> a chaplain and a long-time friend of Weirob's;
> Dave Cohen is a former student of hers.

THE FIRST NIGHT

COHEN: I can hardly believe what you say, Gretchen. You are lucid and do not appear to be in great pain. And yet you say things are hopeless?

WEIROB: These devices can keep me alive for another day or two at most. Some of my vital organs have been injured beyond anything the doctors know how to repair, apart from certain rather radical measures I have rejected. I am not in much pain. But as I under-stand it that is not a particularly good sign. My brain was uninjured and I guess that's why I am as lucid as I ever am. The whole situation is a bit depressing, I fear. But here's Sam Miller. Perhaps he will know how to cheer me up.

MILLER: Good evening, Gretchen. Hello, Dave. I guess there's not much point in beating around the bush, Gretchen; the medics tell me you're a goner. Is there anything I can do to help?

WEIROB: Crimenetley, Sam! You deal with the dying every day. Don't you have anything more comforting to say than

1

"Sorry to hear you're a goner"?

MILLER: Well, to tell you the truth, I'm a little at a loss for what to say to you. Most people I deal with are believers like I am. We talk of the prospects for survival. I give assurance that God, who is just and merciful, would not permit such a travesty as that our short life on this earth should be the end of things. But you and I have talked about religious and philosophical issues for years. I have never been able to find in you the least inclination to believe in God; indeed, it's a rare day when you are sure that your friends have minds, or that you can see your own hand in front of your face, or that there is any reason to believe that the sun will rise tomorrow. How can I hope to comfort you with the prospect of life after death, when I know you will regard it as having no probability whatsoever?

WEIROB: I would not require so much to be comforted, Sam. Even the possibility of something quite improbable can be comforting, in certain situations. When we used to play tennis, I beat you no more than one time in twenty. But this was enough to establish the possibility of beating you on any given occasion, and by focusing merely on the possibility I remained eager to play. Entombed in a secure prison, thinking our situation quite hopeless, we may find unutterable joy in the information that there is, after all, the slimmest possibility of escape. Hope provides comfort, and hope does not always require probability. But we must believe that what we hope for is at least possible. So I will set an easier task for you. Simply persuade me that my survival after the death of this body is *possible*, and I promise to be comforted. Whether you succeed or not, your attempts will be a diversion, for you know I like to talk philosophy more than anything else.

MILLER: But what is possibility, if not reasonable probability?

WEIROB: I do not mean possible in the sense of likely, or even in the sense of conforming to the known laws of physics or biology. I mean possible only in the weakest sense—of being conceivable, given the unavoidable facts. Within the next couple of days, this body will die. It will be buried and it will rot away. I ask that, given these facts, you explain to me how it even makes *sense* to talk of me continuing to exist. Just explain to me what it is I am to *imagine*, when I imagine surviving, that is consistent with these facts, and I shall be comforted.

MILLER: But then what is there to do? There are many conceptions of immortality, of survival past the grave, which all seem to make good sense. Surely not the possibility, but only the probability, can be doubted. Take your choice! Christians believe in life, with a body, in some Hereafter—the details vary, of course, from sect to sect. There is the Greek idea of the body as a prison, from which we escape at death—so that we have continued life without a body. Then there are conceptions in which, so to speak, we merge with the flow of being—

WEIROB: I must cut short your lesson in comparative religion. Survival means surviving, no more, no less. I have no doubts that I shall merge with being; plants will take root in my remains, and the chemicals that I am will continue to make their contribution to life. I am enough of an ecologist to be comforted. But survival, if it is anything, must offer comforts of a different sort, the comforts of *anticipation*. Survival means that tomorrow, or sometime in the future, there will be someone who will experience, who will see and touch and smell—or at the very least, think and reason and remember. And this person will be *me*. This person will be related to me in such a way that it is correct for me to anticipate, to look forward to, those future experiences. And I am related to her in such a way that it will be right for her to remember what I have thought and done, to feel remorse for what I have done wrong, and pride in what I have done right. And the only relation that supports anticipation and memory in this way, is simply *identity*. For it is never correct to anticipate, as happening to oneself, what will happen to someone else, is it? Or to remember, as one's own thoughts and deeds, what someone else did? So don't give me merger with being, or some such nonsense. Give me identity, or let's talk about baseball or fishing—but I'm sorry to get so emotional. I react strongly when words which mean one thing are used for another—when one talks about survival, but does not mean to say that the same person will continue to exist. It's such a sham!

MILLER: I'm sorry. I was just trying to stay in touch with the times, if you want to know the truth, for when I read modern theology or talk to my students who have studied Eastern religions, the notion of survival simply as continued existence of the same person seems out of date. Merger with Being! Merger with Being! That's all I hear. My own beliefs are quite simple, if somewhat vague. I think you will live again—with or without a body, I don't know—I draw comfort from my belief that you and I will be together again, after I also die. We will communicate, somehow. We will continue to grow spiritually. That's what I believe, as surely as I believe that I am sitting here. For I don't know how God could be excused, if this small sample of life is all that we are allotted; I don't know why He should have created us, if these few years of toil and torment are the end of it—

WEIROB: Remember our deal, Sam. You don't have to convince me that survival is probable, for we both agree you would not get to first base. You have only to convince me that it is possible. The only condition is that it be real survival we are talking about, not some up-to-date ersatz survival, which simply amounts to what any ordinary person would call totally ceasing to exist.

MILLER: I guess I just miss the problem, then. Of course, it's possible. You just continue to exist, after your body dies. What's to be defended or explained? You want details? Okay. Two people meet a thousand years from now, in a place that may or may not be part of this physical universe. I am one and you are the other. So you must have survived. Surely you can imagine that. What else is there to say?

WEIROB: But in a few days *I* will quit breathing, *I* will be put into a coffin, *I* will be buried. And in a few months or a few years *I* will be reduced to so much humus. That, I take it, is obvious, is given. How then can you say that I am one of these persons a thousand years from now?

Suppose I took this box of Kleenex and lit fire to it. It is reduced to ashes and I smash the ashes and flush them down the john. Then I say to you, go home and on the shelf will be *that very box of Kleenex*. It has survived! Wouldn't that be absurd? What sense could you make of it? And yet that is just what you say to me. I will rot away. And then, a thousand years later, there I will be. What sense does that make?

MILLER: There could be an *identical* box of Kleenex at your home, one just like it in every respect. And, in this sense, there is no difficulty in there being someone identical to you in the Hereafter, though your body has rotted away.

WEIROB: You are playing with words again. There could be an *exactly similar* box of Kleenex on my shelf. We sometimes use "identical" to mean "exactly similar," as when we speak of "identical twins." But I am using "identical" in a way in which *identity* is the condition of memory and correct anticipation. If I am told that tomorrow, though I will be dead, someone else that looks and sounds and thinks just like me will be alive—would that be comforting? Could I correctly *anticipate* having her experiences? Would it make sense for me to fear her pains and look forward to her pleasures? Would it be right for her to feel remorse at the harsh way I am treating you? Of course not. Similarity, however exact, is not identity. I use identity to mean there is but one thing. If I am to survive, there must be one person who lies in this bed now, and who talks to someone in your Hereafter ten or a thousand years from now. After all, what comfort could there be in the notion of a heavenly imposter, walking around getting credit for the few good things I have done?

MILLER: I'm sorry. I see that I was simply confused. Here is what I should have said. If you were merely a live human body—as the Kleenex box is merely cardboard and glue in a certain arrangement—then the death of your body would be the end of you. But surely you are more than that, fundamentally more than that. What is fundamentally you is not your body, but your soul or self or mind.

WEIROB: Do you mean these words, "soul," "self," or "mind" to come to the same thing?

MILLER: Perhaps distinctions could be made, but I shall not pursue them now. I mean the nonphysical and nonmaterial aspects of you, your consciousness. It is this that I get at with these words, and I don't think any further distinction is relevant.

WEIROB: Consciousness? I am conscious, for a while yet. I see, I hear, I think, I remember. But "to be conscious"— that is a verb. What is the subject of the verb, the thing which is conscious? Isn't it just this body, the same object that is overweight, injured, and lying in bed?—and which will be buried and not be conscious in a day or a week at the most?

MILLER: As you are a philosopher, I would expect you to be less muddled about these issues. Did Descartes not draw a clear distinction between the body and the mind, between that which is overweight, and that which is conscious? Your mind or soul is immaterial, lodged in your body while you are on earth. The two are intimately related but not identical. Now clearly, what concerns us in survival is your mind or soul. It is this which must be identical to the person before me now, and to the one I expect to see in a thousand years in heaven.

WEIROB: So I am not really this body, but a soul or mind or spirit? And this soul cannot be seen or felt or touched or smelt? That is implied, I take it, by the fact that it is immaterial?

MILLER: That's right. Your soul sees and smells, but cannot be seen or smelt.

WEIROB: Let me see if I understand you. You would admit that I am the very same person with whom you had lunch last week at Dorsey's?

MILLER: Of course you are.

WEIROB: Now when you say I am the same person, if I understand you, that is not a remark about this body you see and could touch and I fear can smell. Rather it is a remark about a soul, which you cannot see or touch or smell. The fact that the same body that now lies in front of you on the bed was across the table from you at Dorsey's—that would not mean that the same person was present on both occasions, if the same soul were not. And if, through some strange turn of events, the same soul were present on both occasions, but lodged in different bodies, then it would be the same person. Is that right?

MILLER: You have understood me perfectly. But surely, you understood all of this before!

WEIROB: But wait. I can repeat it, but I'm not sure I understand it. If you cannot see or touch or in any way perceive my soul, what makes you think the one you are confronted with now *is* the very same soul you were confronted with at Dorsey's?

MILLER: But I just explained. To say it is the same soul and to say it is the same person, are the same. And, of course, you are the same person you were before. Who else would you be if not yourself? You *were* Gretchen Weirob, and you *are* Gretchen Weirob.

WEIROB: But how do you know you are talking to Gretchen Weirob at all, and not someone else, say Barbara Walters or even Mark Spitz!

MILLER: Well, it's just obvious. I can see who I am talking to.

WEIROB: But all you can see is my body. You can see, perhaps, that the same body is before you now that was before you last week at Dorsey's. But you have just said that Gretchen Weirob is not a body but a soul. In judging that the same person is before you now as was before you then, you must be making a judgment about souls—which, you said, cannot be seen or touched or smelt or tasted. And so, I repeat, how do you know?

MILLER: Well, I *can* see that it is the same body before me now that was across the table at Dorsey's. And I know that the same soul is connected with the body now that was connected with it before. That's how I know it's you. I see no difficulty in the matter.

WEIROB: You reason on the principle, "Same body, same self."

MILLER: Yes.

WEIROB: And would you reason conversely also? If there were in this bed Barbara Walters' body—that is, the body you see every night on the news—would you infer that it was not me, Gretchen Weirob, in the bed?

MILLER: Of course I would. How would you have come by Barbara Walters' body?

WEIROB: But then merely extend this principle to Heaven, and you will see that your conception of survival is without sense. Surely this very body, which will be buried and as I must so often repeat, *rot away*, will not be in your Hereafter. Different body, different person. Or do you claim that a body can rot away on earth, and then still wind up somewhere else? Must I bring up the Kleenex box again?

MILLER: No, I do not claim that. But I also do not extend a principle, found reliable on earth, to such a different situation as is represented by the Hereafter. That a correlation between bodies and souls has been found on earth does not make it inconceivable or impossible that they should separate. Principles found to work in one circumstance may not be assumed to work in vastly altered circumstances. January and snow go together here, and one would be a fool to expect otherwise. But the principle does not apply in southern California.

WEIROB: So the principle, "same body, same soul," is a well-confirmed regularity, not something you know "a priori."

MILLER: By "a priori" you philosophers mean something which can be known without observing what actually goes on in the world—as I can know that two plus two equals four just by thinking about numbers, and that no bachelors are married, just by thinking about the meaning of "bachelor"?

WEIROB: Yes.

MILLER: Then you are right. If it was part of the meaning of "same body" that wherever we have the same body we have the same soul, it would have to obtain universally, in Heaven as well as on earth. But I just claim it is a generalization we know by observation on earth, and it need not automatically extend to Heaven.

WEIROB: But where do you get this principle? It simply amounts to a correlation between being confronted with the same body and being confronted with the same soul. To establish such a correlation in the first place, surely one must have some *other* means of judging sameness of soul. You do not have such a means; your principle is without foundation; either you really do not know the person before you now is Gretchen Weirob, the very same person you lunched with at Dorsey's, or what you do know has nothing to do with sameness of some immaterial soul.

MILLER: Hold on, hold on. You know I can't follow you when you start spitting out arguments like that. Now what is this terrible fallacy I'm supposed to have committed?

WEIROB: I'm sorry. I get carried away. Here—by way of a peace offering—have one of the chocolates Dave brought.

MILLER: Very tasty. Thank you.

WEIROB: Now why did you choose that one?

MILLER: Because it had a certain swirl on the top which shows that it is a caramel.

WEIROB: That is, a certain sort of swirl is correlated with a certain type of filling—the swirls with caramel, the rosettes with orange, and so forth.

MILLER: Yes. When you put it that way, I see an analogy. Just as I judged that the filling would be the same in this piece as in the last piece that I ate with such a swirl, so I judge that the soul with which I am conversing is the same as the last soul with which I conversed when sitting across from that body. We *see* the outer wrapping and infer what is inside.

WEIROB: But how did you come to realize that swirls of that sort and caramel insides were so associated?

MILLER: Why, from eating a great many of them over the years. Whenever I bit into a candy with that sort of swirl, it was filled with caramel.

WEIROB: Could you have established the correlation had you never been allowed to bite into a candy and never seen what happened when someone else bit into one? You could have formed the hypothesis, "same swirl, same filling." But could you have ever established it?

MILLER: It seems not.

WEIROB: So your inference, in a particular case, to the identity of filling from the identity of swirl would be groundless?

MILLER: Yes, it would. I think I see what is coming.

WEIROB: I'm sure you do. Since you can never, so to speak, bite into my soul, can never see or touch it, you have no way of testing your hypothesis that sameness of body means sameness of self.

MILLER: I daresay you are right. But now I'm a bit lost. What is supposed to follow from all of this?

WEIROB: If, as you claim, identity of persons consisted in identity of immaterial unobservable souls, then judgments of personal identity of the sort we make every day whenever we greet a friend or avoid a pest are really judgments about such souls.

MILLER: Right.

WEIROB: But if such judgments were really about souls, they
           would all be groundless and without foundation. For
           we have no direct method of observing sameness of
           soul, and so—and this is the point made by the candy
           example—we can have no indirect method either.

MILLER: That seems fair.

WEIROB: But our judgments about persons are not all simply
           groundless and silly, so we must not be judging of
           immaterial souls after all.

MILLER: Your reasoning has some force. But I suspect the
           problem lies in my defense of my position, and not
           the position itself. Look here—there *is* a way to test
           the hypothesis of a correlation after all. When I
           entered the room, I expected you to react just as
           you did—argumentatively and skeptically. Had the
           person with this body reacted completely differently
           perhaps I would have been forced to conclude it was
           not you. For example, had she complained about
           not being able to appear on the six o'clock news, and
           missing Harry Reasoner, and so forth, I might eventu-
           ally have been persuaded it *was* Barbara Walters
           and not you. Similarity of psychological characteris-
           tics—a person's attitudes, beliefs, memories, prejudic-
           es, and the like—is observable. These are correlated
           with identity of body on the one side, and of course
           with sameness of soul on the other. So the correla-
           tion between body and soul can be established after
           all by this intermediate link.

WEIROB: And how do you know that?

MILLER: Know what?

WEIROB: That where we have sameness of psychological
           characteristics, we have sameness of soul.

MILLER: Well, now you are really being just silly. The soul or mind is just that which is responsible for one's character, memory, belief. These are aspects of the mind, just as one's height, weight, and appearance are aspects of the body.

WEIROB: Let me grant for the sake of argument that belief, character, memory, and so forth are states of mind. That is, I suppose, I grant that what one thinks and feels is due to the states one's mind is in at that time. And I shall even grant that a mind is an immaterial thing—though I harbor the gravest doubts that this is so. I do not see how it follows that similarity of such traits requires, or is evidence to the slightest degree, for identity of the mind or soul.

            Let me explain my point with an analogy. If we were to walk out of this room, down past the mill and out towards Wilbur, what would we see?

MILLER: We would come to the Blue River, among other things.

WEIROB: And how would you recognize the Blue River? I mean, of course if you left from here, you would scarcely expect to hit the Platte or Niobrara. But suppose you were actually lost, and came across the Blue River in your wandering, just at that point where an old dam partly blocks the flow. Couldn't you recognize it?

MILLER: Yes, I'm sure as soon as I saw that part of the river I would again know where I was.

WEIROB: And how would you recognize it?

MILLER: Well, the turgid brownness of the water, the sluggish flow, the filth washed up on the banks, and such.

WEIROB: In a word, the states of the water which makes up the river at the time you see it.

MILLER: Right.

WEIROB: If you saw blue clean water, with bass jumping, you would know it wasn't the Blue River.

MILLER: Of course.

WEIROB: So you expect, each time you see the Blue, to see the water, which makes it up, in similar states—not always exactly the same, for sometimes it's a little dirtier, but by and large similar.

MILLER: Yes, but what do you intend to make of this?

WEIROB: Each time you see the Blue, it consists of *different* water. The water that was in it a month ago may be in Tuttle Creek Reservoir or in the Mississippi or in the Gulf of Mexico by now. So the *similarity* of states of water, by which you judge the sameness of river, does not require *identity* of the water which is in those states at these various times.

MILLER: And?

WEIROB: And so just because you judge as to personal identity by reference to similarity of states of mind, it does not follow that the mind, or soul, is the same in each case. My point is this. For all you know, the immaterial soul which you think is lodged in my body might change from day to day, from hour to hour, from minute to minute, replaced each time by another soul psychologically similar. You cannot see it or touch it, so how would you know?

MILLER: Are you saying I don't really know who you are?

WEIROB: Not at all. *You* are the one who say personal identity consists in sameness of this immaterial, unobservable, invisible, untouchable soul. I merely point out that *if* it did consist in that, you *would* have no idea who I am. Sameness of body would not necessarily mean

sameness of person. Sameness of psychological characteristics would not necessarily mean sameness of
person. I am saying that if you do know who I am
then you are wrong that personal identity consists
in sameness of immaterial soul.

MILLER: I see. But wait. I believe my problem is that I simply
forgot a main tenet of my theory. The correlation can
be established in my own case. I know that *my* soul
and my body are intimately and consistently found
together. From this one case I can generalize, at least
as concerns life in this world, that sameness of body
is a reliable sign of sameness of soul. This leaves me
free to regard it as intelligible, in the case of death,
that the link between the particular soul and the
particular body it has been joined with is broken.

WEIROB: This would be quite an extrapolation, wouldn't it,
from one case directly observed, to a couple of bil-
lion in which only the body is observed? For I take it
that we are in the habit of assuming, for every person
now on earth, as well as those who have already
come and gone, that the principle "one body, one
soul" is in effect.

MILLER: This does not seem an insurmountable obstacle.
Since there is nothing special about my case, I assume
the arrangement I find in it applies universally until
given some reason to believe otherwise. And I never
have been.

WEIROB: Let's let that pass. I have another problem that is
more serious. How is it that you know in your own
case that there is a single soul which has been so
consistently connected with your body?

MILLER: Now you really cannot be serious, Gretchen. How
can I doubt that I am the same person I was? Is there
anything more clear and distinct, less susceptible to
doubt? How do you expect me to prove anything to
you, when you are capable of denying my own

continued existence from second to second? Without knowledge of our own identity, everything we think and do would be senseless. How could I think if I did not suppose that the person who begins my thought is the one who completes it? When I act, do I not assume that the person who forms the intention is the very one who performs the action?

WEIROB: But I grant you that a single *person* has been associated with your body since you were born. The question is whether one immaterial soul has been so associated—or more precisely, whether you are in a position to know it. You believe that a judgment that one and the same person has had your body all these many years is a judgment that one and the same immaterial soul has been lodged in it. I say that such judgments concerning the soul are totally mysterious, and that if our knowledge of sameness of persons consisted in knowledge of sameness of immaterial soul, it too would be totally mysterious. To point out, as you do, that it is not mysterious, but perhaps the most secure knowledge we have, the foundation of all reason and action, is simply to make the point that it cannot consist of knowledge of identity of an immaterial soul.

MILLER: You have simply asserted, and not established, that my judgment that a single soul has been lodged in my body these many years is mysterious.

WEIROB: Well, consider these possibilities. One is that a single soul, one and the same, has been with this body I call mine since it was born. The other is that one soul was associated with it until five years ago and then another, psychologically similar, inheriting all the old memories and beliefs, took over. A third hypothesis is that every five years a new soul takes over. A fourth is that every five minutes a new soul takes over. The most radical is that there is a constant flow of souls through this body, each psychologically similar to the preceding, as there is a constant flow of water molecules down the Blue. What evidence do I have that the first hypothesis, the "single soul hypothesis" is true, and not one of the others? Because I am the same person I was five minutes or five years ago? But the issue in question is simply whether from sameness of person, which isn't in doubt, we can infer sameness of soul. Sameness of body? But how do I establish a stable relationship between soul and body? Sameness of thoughts and sensations? But they are in constant flux. By the nature of the case, if the soul cannot be observed, it cannot be observed to be the same. Indeed, no sense has ever been assigned to the phrase "same soul." Nor could any sense be attached to it! One would have to say what a single soul looked like or felt like, how an encounter with a single soul at different times differed from encounters with different souls. But this can hardly be done, since a soul according to your conception doesn't look or feel like *anything* at all. And so of course "souls" can afford no principle of identity. And so they cannot be used to bridge the gulf between my existence now and my existence in the hereafter.

MILLER: Do you doubt the existence of your own soul?

WEIROB: I haven't based my argument on there being no immaterial souls of the sort you describe, but merely on their total irrelevance to questions of personal identity, and so to questions of personal survival. I do indeed harbor grave doubts whether there are any immaterial souls of the sort to which you appeal. Can we have a notion of a soul unless we have a notion of the *same* soul? But I hope you do not think that means I doubt my own existence. I think I lie here, overweight and conscious. I think you can see me, not just some outer wrapping, for I think I am just a live human body. But that is not the basis of my argument. I give you these souls. I merely observe that they can by their nature provide no principle of personal identity.

MILLER: I admit I have no answer.

I'm afraid I do not comfort you, though I have perhaps provided you with some entertainment. Emerson said that a little philosophy turns one away from religion, but that deeper understanding brings one back. I know no one who has thought so long and hard about philosophy as you have. Will it never lead you back to a religious frame of mind?

WEIROB: My former husband used to say that a little philosophy turns one away from religion, and more philosophy makes one a pain in the neck. Perhaps he was closer to the truth than Emerson.

MILLER: Perhaps he was. But perhaps by tomorrow night I will have come up with a better argument.

WEIROB: I hope I live to hear it.

THE SECOND NIGHT

WEIROB: Well, Sam, have you figured out a way to make sense of the identity of immaterial souls?

MILLER: No, I have decided it was a mistake to build my argument on such a dubious notion.

WEIROB: Have you then given up on survival? I think such a position would be a hard one for a clergyman to live with, and would feel bad about having pushed you so far.

MILLER: Don't worry. I'm more convinced than ever. I stayed up late last night thinking and reading, and I'm sure I can convince you now.

WEIROB: Get with it, time is running out.

MILLER: First, let me explain why, independently of my desire to defend survival after death, I am dissatisfied with your view that personal identity is just bodily identity. My argument will be very similar to the one you used to convince me that personal identity could not be identified with identity of an immaterial soul.

Consider a person waking up tomorrow morning, conscious, but not yet ready to open her eyes and look around and, so to speak, let the new day officially begin.

WEIROB: Such a state is familiar enough, I admit.

MILLER: Now couldn't such a person tell who she was? That is, even before opening her eyes and looking around, and in particular before looking at her body or making any judgments about it, wouldn't she be able to say who she was? Surely most of us, in the morning, know who we are before opening our eyes and recognizing our own bodies, do we not?

WEIROB: You seem to be right about that.

MILLER: But such a judgment as this person makes—we shall suppose she judges "I am Gretchen Weirob"—*is* a judgment of personal identity. Suppose she says to herself, "I am the very person who was arguing with Sam Miller last night." This is clearly a statement about her identity with someone who was alive the night before. And she could make this judgment without examining her body at all. You could have made just this judgment this morning, before opening your eyes.

WEIROB: Well, in fact I did so. I remembered our conversation of last night and said to myself, "Could I be the rude person who was so hard on Sam Miller's attempts to comfort me?" And, of course, my answer was that I not only could be but was that very rude person.

MILLER: But then by the same principle you used last night personal identity cannot be bodily identity. For you said that it could not be identity of immaterial soul because we were not judging as to identity of immaterial soul when we judge as to personal identity. But by the same token, as my example shows, we are not judging as to bodily identity when we judge as to personal identity. For we can judge who we are, and that we are the very person who did such and such and so and so, without having to make any judgments at all about the body. So, personal identity, while it may not consist of identity of an immaterial soul, does not consist in identity of material body either.

WEIROB: I did argue as you remember. But I also said that the notion of the identity of an immaterial unobservable unextended soul seemed to make no sense at all. This is one reason that cannot be what we are judging about, when we judge as to personal identity. Bodily identity at least makes sense. Perhaps we are assuming sameness of body, without looking.

MILLER: Granted. But you do admit·that we do not in our own cases actually need to make a judgment of bodily identity in order to make a judgment of personal identity?

WEIROB: I don't think I will admit it. I will let it pass, so that we may proceed.

MILLER: Okay. Now it seems to me we are even able to imagine awakening and finding ourselves to have a *different* body than the one we had before. Suppose yourself just as I have described you. And now suppose you finally open your eyes and see, not the body you have grown so familiar with over the years, but one of a fundamentally different shape and size.

WEIROB: Well, I should suppose I had been asleep for a very long time and lost a lot of weight—perhaps I was in a coma for a year or so.

MILLER: But isn't it at least conceivable that it should not be your old body at all? I seem to be able to imagine awakening with a totally new body.

WEIROB: And how would you suppose that this came about?

MILLER: That's beside the point. I'm not saying I can imagine a procedure that would bring this about. I'm saying I can imagine it happening to me. In Kafka's *Metamorpheses*, someone awakens as a cockroach. I can't imagine what would make this happen to me or anyone else, but I can imagine awakening with the body of a cockroach. It is incredible that it should happen—that I do not deny. I simply mean I can imagine experiencing it. It doesn't seem contradictory or incoherent, simply unlikely and inexplicable.

WEIROB: So, if I admit this can be imagined, what follows then?

MILLER: Well, I think it follows that personal identity does not just amount to bodily identity. For I would not, finding that I had a new body, conclude that I was not the very same person I was before. I would be the same *person*, though I did not have the same *body*. So we would have identity of person but not identity of body. So personal identity cannot just amount to bodily identity.

WEIROB: Well suppose—and I emphasize *suppose*—I grant you all of this. Where does it leave you? What do you claim I have recognized as the same, if not my body and not my immaterial soul?

MILLER: I don't claim that you have recognized anything as the same, except the person involved, that is, you yourself.

WEIROB: I'm not sure what you mean.

MILLER: Let me appeal as you did to the Blue River. Suppose I take a visitor to the stretch of river by the old Mill, and then drive him toward Manhattan. After an hour-or-so drive we see another stretch of river, and I say, "That's the same river we saw this morning." As you pointed out yesterday, I don't thereby imply that the very same molecules of water are seen both times. And the places are different, perhaps a hundred miles apart. And the shape and color and level of pollution might all be different. What do I see later in the day that is identical with what I saw earlier in the day?

WEIROB: Nothing except the river itself.

MILLER: Exactly. But now notice that what I see, strictly speaking, is not the whole river but only a part of it. I see different parts of the same river at the two different times. So really, if we restrict ourselves to what I literally see, I do not judge identity at all, but something else.

WEIROB: And what might that be?

MILLER: In saying that the river seen earlier, and the river seen later, are one and the same river, do I mean any more than that the stretch of water seen later and that stretch of water seen earlier are connected by other stretches of water?

WEIROB: That's about right. If the stretches of water are so connected there is but one river of which they are both parts.

MILLER: Yes, that's what I mean. The statement of identity, "This river is the same one we saw this morning," is in a sense about rivers. But in a way it is also about stretches of water or river parts.

WEIROB: So is all of this something special about rivers?

MILLER: Not at all. It is a recurring pattern. After all, we constantly deal with objects extended in space and time. But we are seldom aware of the objects' wholes, but only of their parts or stretches of their histories. When a statement of identity is not just something trivial, like "This bed is this bed," it is usually because we are really judging that different parts fit together, in some appropriate pattern, into a certain kind of whole.

WEIROB: I'm not sure I see just what you mean yet.

MILLER: Let me give you another example. Suppose we are sitting together watching the first game of a double-header. You ask me, "Is this game identical with this game?" This is a perfectly stupid question, though, of course, strictly speaking it makes sense and the answer is "yes."

But now suppose you leave in the sixth inning to go for hot dogs. You are delayed, and return after about forty-five minutes or so. You ask, "Is this the same game I was watching?" Now your question is not stupid, but perfectly appropriate.

WEIROB: Because the first game might still be going on or it might have ended, and the second game begun, by the time I return.

MILLER: Exactly. Which is to say somehow different parts of the game—different innings, or at least different plays—were somehow involved in your question. That's why it wasn't stupid or trivial but significant.

WEIROB: So, you think that judgments as to the identity of an object of a certain kind—rivers or baseball games or whatever—involve judgments as to the *parts* of those things being connected in a certain way, and are significant only when different parts are involved. Is that your point?

MILLER: Yes, and I think it is an important one. How foolish it would be, when we ask a question about the identity of baseball games, to look for something *else*, other than the game as a whole, which had to be the same. It could be the same game, even if different players were involved. It could be the same game, even if it had been moved to a different field. These other things, the innings, the plays, the players, the field, don't have to be the same at the different times for the game to be the same, they just have to be related in certain ways so as to make that complex whole we call a single game.

WEIROB: You think we were going off on a kind of a wild-goose chase when we asked whether it was the identity of soul or body that was involved in the identity of persons?

MILLER: Yes. The answer I should now give is neither. We are wondering about the identity of the person. Of course, if by "soul" we just mean "person," there is no problem. But if we mean, as I did yesterday, some other thing whose identity is already understood, which has to be the same when persons are the same, we are just fooling ourselves with words.

WEIROB: With rivers and baseball games, I can see that they are made up of parts connected in a certain way. The connection is, of course, different in the two cases, as is the sort of "part" involved. River parts must be connected physically with other river parts to form a continuous whole. Baseball innings must be connected so that the score, batting order, and the like are carried over from the earlier inning to the later one according to the rules. Is there something analagous we are to say about persons?

MILLER: Writers who concern themselves with this speak of "person-stages." That is just a stretch of consciousness, such as you and I are aware of now. I am aware of a flow of thoughts and feelings that are mine, you are aware of yours. A person is just a whole composed of such stretches as parts, not some substance that underlies them, as I thought yesterday, and not the body in which they occur, as you seem to think. That is the conception of a person I wish to defend today.

WEIROB: So when I awoke and said to myself, "I am the one who was so rude to Sam Miller last night," I was judging that a certain stretch of consciousness I was then aware of, and an earlier one I remembered having been aware of, form a single whole of the appropriate sort—a single stream of consciousness, we might say.

MILLER: Yes, that's it exactly. You need not worry about whether the same immaterial soul is involved, or even whether that makes sense. Nor need you worry about whether the same body is involved, as indeed you do not since you don't even have to open your eyes and look. Identity is not, so to speak, something under the person-stages, nor in something they are attached to, but something you build from them.

Now survival, you can plainly see, is no problem at all once we have this conception of personal identity. All you need suppose is that there is, in Heaven, a conscious being, and that the person-stages that make her up are in the appropriate relation to those that now make you up, so that they are parts of the same whole—namely, you. If so, you have survived. So will you admit now that survival is at least possible?

WEIROB: Hold on, hold on. Comforting me is not that easy. You will have to show that it is possible that these person-stages or stretches of consciousness be related in the appropriate way. And to do that, won't you have to tell me what that way is?

MILLER: Yes, of course. I was getting ahead of myself. It is right at this point that my reading was particularly helpful. In a chapter of his *Essay On Human Understanding* Locke discusses this very question. He suggests that the relation between two person-stages or stretches of consciousness that makes them stages of a single person is just that the later one contains memories of the earlier one. He doesn't say this in so many words—he talks of "extending our consciousness back in time." But he seems to be thinking of memory.

WEIROB: So, any past thought or feeling or intention or desire that I can remember having is mine?

MILLER: That's right. I can remember only my own past thoughts and feelings, and you only yours. Of course, everyone would readily admit that. Locke's insight is to take this relation as the source of identity and not just its consequence. To remember—or more plausibly, to be able to remember—the thoughts and feelings of a person who was conscious in the past is just what it is to be that person.

Now you can easily see that this solves the problem of the possibility of survival. As I was saying, all you need to do is imagine someone at some future time, not on this earth and not with your present thoughts and feelings, remembering the very conversation we are having now. This does not require sameness of anything else, but it amounts to sameness of person. So, now will you admit it?

WEIROB: No, I don't.

MILLER: Well, what's the problem now?

WEIROB: I admit that if I remember having a certain thought or feeling had by some person in the past, then I must indeed be that person. Though I can remember watching others think, I cannot remember their thinking, any more than I can experience it at the time it occurs if it is theirs and not mine. This is the kernel of Locke's idea, and I don't see that I could deny it.

But we must distinguish—as I'm sure you will agree—between *actually* remembering and merely *seeming* to remember. Many men who think that they are Napoleon claim to remember losing the battle of Waterloo. We may suppose them to be sincere, and to really seem to remember it. But they do not actually remember because they were not at the battle and are not Napoleon.

MILLER: Of course I admit that we must distinguish between actually remembering and only seeming to.

WEIROB: And you will admit too, I trust, that the thought of some person at some far place and some distant time seeming to remember this conversation I am having with you would not give me the sort of comfort that the prospect of survival is supposed to provide. I would have no reason to anticipate future experiences of this person, simply because she is to *seem* to remember my experiences. The experiences of such a deluded imposter are not ones I can look forward to having.

MILLER: I agree.

WEIROB: So the mere possibility of someone in the future

seeming to remember this conversation does not show the possibility of my surviving. Only the possibility of someone actually remembering this conversation—or, to be precise, the experiences I am having—would show that.

MILLER: Of course. But what are you driving at? Where is the problem? I can imagine someone being deluded, but also someone actually being you and remembering your present thoughts.

WEIROB: But, what's the difference? How do you know *which* of the two you are imagining, and *what* you have shown possible?

MILLER: Well, I just imagine the one and not the other. I don't see the force of your argument.

WEIROB: Let me try to make it clear with another example. Imagine two persons. One is talking to you, saying certain words, having certain thoughts, and so forth. The other is not talking to you at all, but is in the next room being hypnotized. The hypnotist gives to this person a post-hypnotic suggestion that upon awakening he will remember having had certain thoughts and having uttered certain words to you. The thoughts and words he mentions happen to be just the thoughts and words which the first person actually thinks and says. Do you understand the situation?

MILLER: Yes, continue.

WEIROB: Now, in a while, both of the people are saying sentences which begin, "I remember saying to Sam Miller—" and "I remember thinking as I talked to Sam Miller." And they both report remembering just the same thoughts and utterances. One of these will be remembering and the other only seeming to remember, right?

MILLER: Of course.

WEIROB: Now which one is *actually* remembering?

MILLER: Why, the very one who was in the room talking to me, of course. The other one is just under the influence of the suggestion made by the hypnotist and not remembering talking to me at all.

WEIROB: Now you agree that the difference between them does not consist in the content of what they are now thinking or saying.

MILLER: Agreed. The difference is in the relation to the past thinking and speaking. In the one case the relation of memory obtains. In the other, it does not.

WEIROB: But they both satisfy part of the conditions of remembering, for they both *seem to remember*. So there must be some further condition that the one satisfies and the other does not. I am trying to get you to say what that further condition is.

MILLER: Well, I said that the one who had been in this room talking would be remembering.

WEIROB: In other words, given two putative rememberers of some past thought or action, the real rememberer is the one who, in addition to seeming to remember the past thought or action, actually thought it or did it.

MILLER: Yes.

WEIROB: That is to say, the one who is identical with the person who did the past thinking and uttering.

MILLER: Yes, I admit it.

WEIROB: So, your argument just amounts to this. Survival is possible, because imaginable. It is imaginable, because my identity with some Heavenly person is imaginable. To imagine it, we imagine a person in Heaven who, First, seems to remember my thoughts and actions, and Second, is me.

Surely, there could hardly be a tighter circle. If I have doubts that the Heavenly person is me, I will have doubts as to whether she is really remembering or only seeming to. No one could doubt the possibility of some future person who, after death, seemed to remember the things he thought and did. But that possibility does not resolve the issue about the possibility of survival. Only the possibility of someone *actually* remembering could do that—for that, as we agree, is sufficient for identity. But doubts about survival and identity simply go over without remainder into doubts about whether the memories would be actual or merely apparent. You guarantee me no more than the possibility of a deluded Heavenly imposter.

COHEN: But wait, Gretchen. I think Sam was less than fair to his own idea just now.

WEIROB: You think you can break out of the circle of using real memory to explain identity, and identity to mark the difference between real and apparent memory? Feel free to try.

COHEN: Let us return to your case of the hypnotist. You point out that we have two putative rememberers. You ask what marks the difference, and claim the answer must be the circular one—that the real rememberer is the person who actually had the experiences both seem to remember.

But that is not the only possible answer. The experiences themselves cause the later apparent memories in the one case, while the hypnotist causes them in the other. We can say that the rememberer is the one of the two whose memories were *caused in the right way* by the earlier experiences. We thus distinguish between the rememberer and the hypnotic subject, without appeal to identity.

The idea that real memory amounts to apparent memory plus identity is misleading anyway. I seem to remember, as a small child, knocking over the Menorah so the candles fell into and spoiled a tureen of soup. And I did actually perform such a feat. So we have apparent memory and identity. But I do *not* actually remember; I was much too young when I did this to remember it now. I have simply been told the story so often I seem to remember.

Here the suggestion that real memory is apparent memory that was caused in the appropriate way by the past events fares better. Not my experience of pulling over the Menorah, but hearing my parents talk about it later, caused my memory-like impressions.

WEIROB: You analyze personal identity into memory, and memory into apparent memory which is caused in the right way. A person is a certain sort of causal process.

COHEN: Right.

WEIROB: Suppose now for the sake of argument I accept this. How does it help Sam in his defense of the possibility of survival? In ordinary memory, the causal chain from remembered event to memory of it never leads us outside the confines of a single body. Indeed, the normal process of which you speak surely involves storage of information somehow in the brain. How can the states of my brain, when I die, influence in the appropriate way the apparent memories of the Heavenly person Sam takes to be me?

COHEN: Well, I didn't intend to be defending the possibility of survival. That is Sam's problem. I just like the idea that personal identity can be explained in terms of memory, and not just in terms of identity of the body.

MILLER: But surely, this does provide me with the basis for further defense. Your challenge, Gretchen, was to explain the difference between two persons in Heaven, one who actually remembers your experience—and so is you—and one who simply seems to remember it. But can I not just say that the one who is you is the one whose states were caused in the appropriate way? I do not mean the way they would be in a normal case of earthly memory. But in the case of the Heavenly being who is you, God would have created her with the brain states (or whatever) she has *because* you had the ones you had at death. Surely it is not the exact form of the dependence of my later memories on my earlier perceptions that makes them really memories, but the fact that the process involved has preserved information.

WEIROB: So if God creates a Heavenly person, designing her brain to duplicate the brain I have upon death, that person is me. If, on the other hand, a Heavenly being should come to be with those very same memory-like states by accident (if there are accidents in Heaven) it would not be me.

MILLER: Exactly. Are you satisfied now that survival makes perfectly good sense?

WEIROB: No, I'm still quite unconvinced.
           The problem I see is this. If God could create one person in Heaven, and by designing her after me, make her me, why could he not make two such bodies, and cause this transfer of information into both of them? Would both of these Heavenly persons then be me? It seems as clear as anything in philosophy that from

A is B

and

C is B

where by "is" we mean identity, we can infer,

A is C.

So, if each of these Heavenly persons is me, they must be each other. But then they are not two but one. But my assumption was that God creates two, not one. He could create them physically distinct, capable of independent movement, perhaps in widely separated Heavenly locations, each with her own duties to perform, her own circle of Heavenly friends, and the like.

So either God, by creating a Heavenly person with a brain modeled after mine, does not really create someone identical with me but merely someone similar to me, or God is somehow limited to making only one such being. I can see no reason why, if there were a God, He should be so limited. So I take the first option. He could create someone similar to me, but not someone who would *be* me. Either your analysis of memory is wrong, and such a being does not, after all, remember what I am doing or saying, or memory is not sufficient for personal identity. Your theory has gone wrong somewhere, for it leads to absurdity.

COHEN: But wait. Why can't Sam simply say that if God makes one such creature, she is you, while if he makes more, none of them is you? It's possible that he makes only one. So it's possible that you survive. Sam always meant to allow that it's *possible* that you won't survive. He had in mind the case in which there is no God to make the appropriate Heavenly persons, or God exists, but doesn't make even one. You have simply shown that there is another way of not surviving. Instead of making too few Heavenly rememberers, He makes too many. So what? He might make the right number, and then you would survive.

WEIROB: Your remarks really amount to a change in your position. Now you are not claiming that memory alone is enough for personal identity. Now, it is memory *plus* lack of competition, the absence of other rememberers, that is needed for personal identity.

COHEN: It does amount to a change of position. But what of it? Is there anything untenable about the position as changed?

WEIROB: Let's look at this from the point of view of the Heavenly person. She says to herself, "Oh, I must be Gretchen Weirob, for I remember doing what she did and saying what she said." But now that's a pretty tenuous conclusion, isn't it? She is really only entitled to say, "Oh, either I'm Gretchen Weirob, or God has created more than one being like me, and none of us is." Identity has become something dependent on things wholly extrinsic to her. Who she is now turns on not just her states of mind and their relation to my states of mind, but on the existence or nonexistence of other people. Is this really what you want to maintain?

   Or look at it from my point of view. God creates one of me in Heaven. Surely I should be glad if convinced this was to happen. Now he creates another, and I should despair again, for this means I won't survive after all. How can doubling a good deed make it worthless?

COHEN: Are you saying that there is some contradiction in my suggestion that only creation of a unique Heavenly Gretchen counts as your survival?

WEIROB: No, it's not contradictory, as far as I can see. But it seems odd in a way that shows that something somewhere is wrong with your theory. Here is a certain relationship I have with a Heavenly person. There being such a person, to whom I am related in this way, is something that is of great importance to me, a source of comfort. It makes it appropriate for me to anticipate having her experiences, since she is just me. Why should my having that relation to another being destroy my relation to this one? You say because then I will not be identical with either of them.

But since you have provided a theory about what that identity consists in, we can look and see what it amounts to for me to be or not to be identical. If she is to remember my experience, I can rightly anticipate hers. But then it seems the doubling makes no difference. And yet it must, for one cannot be identical with two. So you add, in a purely *ad hoc* manner, that her memory of me isn't enough to make my anticipation of her experiences appropriate, if there are two rather than one so linked. Isn't it more reasonable to conclude, since memory does not secure identity when there are two Heavenly Gretchens, it also doesn't when there is only one?

COHEN: There is something *ad hoc* about it, I admit. But perhaps that's just the way our concept works. You have not elicited a contradiction—

WEIROB: An infinite pile of absurdities has the same weight as a contradiction. And absurdities can be generated without limit from your account. Suppose God created this Heavenly person before I died. Then He in effect kills me; if He has already created her, then you really are not talking to whom you think, but someone new, created by Gretchen Weirob's strange death moments ago. Or suppose He first creates one being in Heaven, who is me. Then He creates another. Does the first cease to be me? If God can create such beings in Heaven, surely He can do so in Albuquerque. And there is nothing on your theory to favor this body before you as Gretchen Weirob's, over the one belonging to the person created in Albuquerque. So I am to suppose that if God were to do this, I would suddenly cease to be. I'm tempted to say I would cease to be Gretchen Weirob. But that would be a confused way of putting it. There would be here, in my place, a new person with false memories of having been Gretchen Weirob, who has just died of competition—a strange death if ever there was one. She would have no right to my name, my bank account, or the services of my doctor, who is paid from insurance premiums paid for by deductions from Gretchen Weirob's past salary. Surely this is nonsense; however carefully God should choose to duplicate me, in Heaven or in Albuquerque, I would not cease to be, or cease to be who I am. You may reply that God, being benevolent, would never create an extra Gretchen Weirob. But I do not say that he would, but only that if he did this would not, as your theory implies, mean that I cease to exist. Your theory gives the wrong answer in this possible circumstance, so it must be wrong. I think I have been given no motivation to abandon the most obvious and straightforward view on these matters. I am a live body, and when that body dies, my existence will be at an end.

THE THIRD NIGHT

WEIROB: Well, Sam, are you here for a third attempt to convince me of the possibility of survival?

MILLER: No, I have given up. I suggest we talk about fishing or football or something unrelated to your imminent demise. You will outwit any straightforward attempts to comfort you, but perhaps I can at least divert your mind.

COHEN: But before we start on fishing—although I don't have any particular brief for survival—there is one point in our discussion of the last two evenings that still bothers me. Would you mind discussing for a while the notion of personal identity itself, without worrying about the more difficult case of survival after death?

WEIROB: I would enjoy it. What point bothers you?

COHEN: Your position seems to be that personal identity amounts to identity of a human body, nothing more, nothing less. A person is just a live human body, or more precisely, I suppose, a human body that is alive and has certain capacities—consciousness and perhaps rationality. Is that right?

WEIROB: Yes, it seems that simple to me.

COHEN: But I think there has actually been an episode which disproves that. I am thinking of the strange case of Julia North, which occurred in California a few months ago. Surely you remember it.

WEIROB: Yes, only too well. But you had better explain it to Sam, for I'll wager he has not heard of it.

COHEN: Not heard of Julia North? But the case was all over the headlines.

MILLER: Well, Gretchen is right. I know nothing of it. She knows that I only read the sports page.

COHEN: You only read the sports page!

WEIROB: It's an expression of his unconcern with earthly matters.

MILLER: Well, that's not quite fair, Gretchen. It's a matter of preference. I much prefer to spend what time I have for reading in reading about the eighteenth century, rather than the drab and miserable century into which I had the misfortune to be born. It was really a much more civilized century, you know. But let's not dwell on my peculiar habits. Tell me about Julia North.

COHEN: Very well. Julia North was a young woman who was run over by a streetcar while saving the life of a young child who wandered onto the tracks. The child's mother, one Mary Frances Beaudine, had a stroke while watching the horrible scene. Julia's healthy brain and wasted body, and Mary Frances' healthy body and wasted brain, were transported to a hospital where a brilliant neurosurgeon, Dr. Matthews, was in residence. He had worked out a procedure for what he called a "body transplant." He removed the brain from Julia's head and placed it in Mary Frances', splicing the nerves, and so forth, using techniques not available until quite recently. The survivor of all of this was obviously Julia, as everyone agreed—except, unfortunately, Mary Frances' husband. His shortsightedness and lack of imagination led to great complications and drama, and made the case more famous in the history of crime than in the history of medicine. I shall not go into the details of this sorry aspect of the case—they are well reported in a book by Barbara Harris called *Who is Julia?*, in case you are interested.

MILLER: Fascinating!

COHEN: Well, the relevance of this case is obvious. Julia North had one body up until the time of the accident, and another body after the operation. So one person had two bodies. So a person cannot be simply *identified* with a human body. So something must be wrong with your view, Gretchen. What do you say to this?

WEIROB: I'll say to you just what I said to Dr. Matthews—

COHEN: You have spoken with Dr. Matthews?

WEIROB: Yes. He contacted me shortly after my accident. My physician had phoned him up about my case. Matthews said he could perform the same operation for me he did for Julia North. I refused.

COHEN: You refused! But Gretchen, why—?

MILLER: Gretchen, I *am* shocked. Your decision practically amounts to suicide! You passed up an opportunity to continue living? Why on earth—

WEIROB: Hold on, hold on. You are both making an assumption I reject. If the case of Julia North amounts to a counterexample to my view that a person is just a live human body, and if my refusal to submit to this procedure amounts to suicide, then the survivor of such an operation must be reckoned as the same person as the brain donor. That is, the survivor of Julia North's operation must have been Julia, and the survivor of the operation on me would have to be me. This is the assumption you both make in criticizing me. But I reject it. I think Jack Beaudine was right. The survivor of the operation involving Julia North's brain was Mary Frances Beaudine, and the survivor of the operation using my brain would not have been me.

MILLER: Gretchen, how on earth can you say that? Will you not give up your view that personal identity is just bodily identity, no matter how clear the counterexample? I really think you simply have an irrational attachment to the lump of material that is your body.

COHEN: Yes, Gretchen, I agree with Sam. You are being preposterous! The survivor of Julia North's operation had no idea who Mary Frances Beaudine was. She remembered being Julia—

WEIROB: She *seemed* to remember being Julia. Have you forgotten so quickly the importance of this distinction? In my opinion, the effect of the operation was that Mary Frances Beaudine survived deluded, thinking she was someone else.

COHEN: But as you know, the case was litigated. It went to the Supreme Court. They said that the survivor was Julia.

WEIROB: That argument is unworthy of you, Dave. Is the Supreme Court infallible?

COHEN: No, it isn't. But I don't think it's such a stupid point.

Look at it this way, Gretchen. This is a case in which two criteria we use to make judgments of identity conflict. Usually we expect personal identity to involve both bodily identity and psychological continuity. That is, we expect that if we have the same body, then the beliefs, memories, character traits, and the like also will be enormously similar. In this case, these two criteria which usually coincide do not. If we choose one criterion, we say that the survivor is Mary Frances Beaudine and she has undergone drastic psychological changes. If we choose the other, we say that Julia has survived with a new body. We have to choose which criterion is more important. It's a matter of choice of how to use our language, how to extend the concept "same person" to a new situation. The overwhelming majority of people involved in the case took the survivor to be Julia. That is, society chose to use the concept one way rather than the other. The Supreme Court is *not* beside the point.

One of their functions is to settle just how old concepts shall be applied to new circumstances—how "freedom of the press" is to be understood when applied to movies or television, whose existence was not forseen when the concept was shaped, or to say whether "murder" is to include the abortion of a fetus. They are fallible on points of fact, but they are the final authority on the development of certain important concepts used in law. The notion of *person* is such a concept.

WEIROB: You think that *who* the survivor was, was a matter of convention, of how we choose to use language?

COHEN: Yes.

WEIROB: I can show the preposterousness of all that with an example.

Let us suppose that I agree to the operation. I lie in bed, expecting my continued existence, anticipating the feelings and thoughts I shall have upon awakening after the operation. Dr. Matthews enters and asks me to take several aspirin, so as not to have a headache when I awake. I protest that aspirin upsets my stomach; he asks whether I would rather have a terrible headache tomorrow or a mild stomachache now, and I agree that it would be reasonable to take them.

Let us suppose that you enter at this point, with bad news. The Supreme Court has changed its mind! So the survivor will not be me. So, I say, "Oh, then I will not take the aspirin, for it's not me that will have a headache, but someone else. Why should I endure a stomachache, however mild, for the comfort of someone else? After all, I am already donating my brain to that person."

Now this is clearly absurd. If I were correct, in the first place, to anticipate having the sensations and thoughts that the survivor is to have the next day, the decision of nine old men a thousand or so miles away wouldn't make me wrong. And if I was wrong to so anticipate, their decision couldn't make me right.

How can the correctness of my anticipation of survival be a matter of the way we use our words? If it is not such a matter, then my identity is not either. My identity with the survivor, my survival, is a question of fact, not of convention.

COHEN: Your example is persuasive. I admit I am befuddled. On the one hand, I cannot see how the matter can be other than I have described. When we know all the facts what can remain to be decided but how we are to describe them, how we are to use our language? And yet I can see that it seems absurd to suppose that the correctness or incorrectness of anticipation of future experience is a matter for convention to decide.

MILLER: Well, I didn't think the business about convention was very plausible anyway. But I should like to return you to the main question, Gretchen. Fact or convention, it still remains. Why will you not admit that the survivor of this operation would be you?

WEIROB: Well, *you* tell *me*, why you think she would be me?

MILLER: I can appeal to the theory I developed last night. You argued that the idea that personal identity consists in memory would not guarantee the possibility of survival after death. But you said nothing to shake its plausibility as an account of personal identity. It has the enormous advantage, remember, of making sense of our ability to judge our own identity, without examination of our bodies. I should argue that it is the correctness of this theory that explains the *almost* universal willingness to say that the survivor of Julia's operation was Julia. We need not deliberate over how to extend our concept, we need only apply the concept we already have. Memory is sufficient for identity and bodily identity is *not* necessary for it. The survivor remembered Julia's thoughts and actions, and so was Julia. Would you but submit to the operation, the survivor would remember your thoughts and actions, would remember this very conversation we are now having, and would be you.

COHEN: Yes, I now agree completely with Sam. The theory that personal identity is to be analyzed in terms of memory is correct, and according to it you will survive if you submit to the operation.

Let me add another argument against your view and in favor of the memory theory. You have emphasized that identity is the condition of *anticipation*. That means, among other things, that we have a particular concern for that person in the future whom we take to be ourselves. If I were told that any of the three of us were to suffer pain tomorrow, I should be sad. But if it were you or Sam that were to be hurt, my concern would be altruistic or unselfish. That is because I would not anticipate having the painful experience myself. Here I do no more than repeat points you have made earlier in our conversations.

Now what is there about mere sameness of body that makes sense of this asymmetry, between the way we look at our own futures, and the way we look at the futures of others? In other words, why is the identity of your body—that mere lump of matter, as Sam put it—of such great importance? Why care so much about it?

WEIROB: You say, and I surely agree, that identity of person is a very special relationship—so special as perhaps not even happily called a relationship at all. And you say that since my theory is that identity of person is identity of body, I should be able to explain the importance of the one in terms of the importance of the other.

I'm not sure I can do that. But does the theory that personal identity consists in memory fare better on this score?

COHEN: Well, I think it does. Those properties of persons which make persons of such great value, and mark their individuality, and make one person so special to his friends and loved ones, are ultimately psychological or mental. One's character, personality, beliefs, attitudes, convictions—they are what make every person so unique and special. A skinny Gretchen would be a shock to us all, but not a Gretchen diminished in any important way. But a Gretchen who was not witty, or not gruff, or not as honest to the path an argument takes as is humanly possible—those would be fundamental changes. Is it any wonder that the survivor of that California fiasco was reckoned as Julia North? Would it make sense to take her to be Mary Jane Beaudine, when she had none of her beliefs or attitudes or memories?

Now if such properties are what is of importance about a person to others, is it not reasonable that they are the basis of one's importance to oneself? And these are just the properties that personal identity preserves when it is taken to consist in links of memory. Do we not have, in this idea, at least the beginning of an explanation of the importance of identity?

WEIROB: So on two counts you two favor the memory theory. First, you say it explains how it is possible to judge as to one's own identity, without having to examine one's body. Second, you say it explains the importance of personal identity.

COHEN: Now surely you must agree the memory theory is correct. Do you agree? There may be still time to contact Dr. Matthews—

WEIROB: Hold on, hold on. Try to relax and enjoy the argument. I am. Quit trying to save my life and worry about saving your theory—for I'm still not persuaded. Granted the survivor will *think* she is me, will *seem* to remember thinking my thoughts. But recall the importance of distinguishing between real and merely apparent memory—

COHEN: But *you* recall that this distinction is to be made on the basis of whether the apparent memories were or were not caused by the prior experiences in the appropriate way. The survivor will not seem to remember your thoughts because of hypnosis or by coincidence or overweening imagination. She will seem to remember them because the traces those experiences left on your brain now activate her mind in the usual way. She will seem to remember them because she does remember them, and will be you.

WEIROB: You are very emphatic, and I'm feeling rather weak. I'm not sure there is time left to untangle all of this. But there is never an advantage to hurrying when doing philosophy. So let's go over this slowly.

We all agree that the fact that the survivor of this strange operation Dr. Matthews proposes would *seem* to remember doing what I have done. Let us even suppose she would take herself to be me, claim to be Gretchen Weirob—and have no idea who else she might be. (We are then assuming that she differs from me in one aspect—her theory of personal identity. But that does not show her not to be me, for I could change my mind by then.) We all first agree that this much does not make her me. For this could all be true of someone suffering a delusion, or a subject of hypnosis.

COHEN: Yes, this is all agreed.

WEIROB: But now you think that some *future* condition is satisfied, which makes her apparent memories *real* memories. Now what exactly is this future condition?

COHEN: Well, that the same brain was involved in the perception of the events, and their later *memory*. Thus we have here a causal chain of just the same sort as when only a single body is involved. That is, perceptions when the event occurs leave a trace in the brain, which is later responsible for the content of the memory. And we agreed, did we not, that apparent memory, caused in the right way, is real memory?

WEIROB: Now is it absolutely crucial that the same brain is involved?

COHEN: What do you mean?

WEIROB: Let me explain again by reference to Dr. Matthews. In our conversation he explained a new procedure on which he was working, called a *brain rejuvenation*. By this process, which is not yet available—only the feasibility of developing it is being studied—a new brain could be made which is an exact duplicate of my brain—that is, an exact duplicate in terms of psychologically relevant states. It might not duplicate all the properties of my brain—for example, the blood vessels in the new brain might be stronger than in the old brain.

MILLER: What is the point of developing such a macabre technique?

WEIROB: Dr. Matthews' idea is that when weaknesses which might lead to stroke or other brain injury are noted, a healthy duplicate could be made to replace the original, forestalling the problem.

           Now Dave, suppose my problem were not with my liver and kidneys and such, but with my brain. Would you recommend such an operation as to my benefit?

COHEN: You mean, do I think the survivor of such an operation would be you?

WEIROB: Exactly. You may assume that Dr. Matthews' technique works perfectly so the causal process involved is no less reliable than that involved in ordinary memory.

COHEN: Then I would say it was you— No! Wait! No, it wouldn't be you—absolutely not.

MILLER: But why the sudden reversal? It seems to me it would be her. Indeed, I should try such an operation myself, if it would clear up my dizzy spells and leave me otherwise unaffected.

COHEN: No, don't you see, she is leading us into a false trap. If we say it *is* her, then she will say, "then what if he makes two duplicates, or three or ten? They can't all be me, they all have an equal claim, so none will be me." It would be the argument of last night, reapplied on earth. So the answer is no, absolutely not, it wouldn't be you. Duplication of brain does not preserve identity. Identity of the person requires identity of the brain.

MILLER: Quite right.

WEIROB: Now let me see if I have managed to understand your theory, for my powers of concentration seem to be fading. Suppose we have two bodies, A and B. My brain is put into A, a duplicate into B. The survivor of this, call them "A-Gretchen" and "B-Gretchen," both seem to remember giving this very speech. Both are in this state of seeming to remember, as the last stage in an information-preserving causal chain, initiated by my giving this speech. Both have my character, personality, beliefs, and the like. But one is *really* remembering, the other is not. A-Gretchen is really me, B-Gretchen is not.

COHEN: Precisely. Is this incoherent?

WEIROB: No, I guess there is nothing incoherent about it. But look what has happened to the advantages you claimed for the memory theory.

First, you said, it explains how I can know who I am without opening my eyes and recognizing my body. But on your theory Gretchen-A and Gretchen-B cannot know who they are even if they do open their eyes and examine their bodies. How is Gretchen-A to know whether she has the original brain and is who she seems to be, or has the duplicate and is a new person, only a few minutes old, and with no memories but mere delusions? If the hospital kept careless records, or the surgeon thought it was of no great importance to keep track of who got the original and who got the duplicate, she might never know who she was. By making identity of person turn into identity of brain, your theory makes the ease with which I can determine who I am not less but more mysterious than my theory.

Second, you said, your theory explains why my concern for Gretchen-A, who is me whether she knows it or not, would be selfish, and my anticipation of her experience correct while my concern for Gretchen-B with her duplicated brain would be unselfish, and my anticipation of having her experiences incorrect. And it explains this, you said, because by insisting on the links of memory, we preserve in personal identity more psychological characteristics which are the most important features of a person.

But Gretchen-A and Gretchen-B are psychologically indiscernible. Though they will go their separate ways, at the moment of awakening they could well be exactly similar in every psychological respect. In terms of character and belief and the contents of their minds, Gretchen-A is no more like me than Gretchen-B. So there is nothing in your theory after all to explain why anticipation is appropriate when we have identity and not otherwise.

You said, Sam, that I had an irrational attachment for this unworthy material object, my body. But you too are as irrationally attached to your brain. I have never seen my brain. I should have easily given it up for a rejuvenated version, had that been the choice with which I was faced. I have never seen it, never felt it, and have no attachment to it. But my body? That seems to me all that I am. I see no point in trying to evade its fate, even if there were still time.

But perhaps I miss the merit of your arguments. I am tired, and perhaps my poor brain, feeling slighted, has begun to desert me—

COHEN: Oh, don't worry, Gretchen, you are still clever. Again you have left me befuddled. I don't know what to say. But answer me this. Suppose you are right and we are wrong. But suppose these arguments had not occurred to you, and, sharing in our error, you had agreed to the operation. You anticipate the operation until it happens, thinking you will survive. You are happy. The survivor takes herself to be you, and thinks she made a decision before the operation which has now turned out to be right. She is happy. Your friends are happy. Who would be worse off, either before or after the operation?

Suppose even that you realize identity would not be preserved by such an operation, but have it done anyway, and as the time for the operation approaches, you go ahead and anticipate the experiences of the survivor. Where exactly is the mistake? Do you really have any less reason to care for the survivor than for yourself? Can mere identity of body, the lack of which alone keeps you from being her, mean that much? Perhaps we were wrong, after all, in focusing on identity as the necessary condition of anticipation—

MILLER: Dave, it's too late.

FOOTNOTES

THE FIRST NIGHT: The arguments against the position that personal identity consists in identity of an immaterial soul are similar to those found in John Locke, "Of Identity and Diversity," chapter 27 of Book II of the *Essay Concerning Human Understanding*. This chapter first appeared in the second edition of 1694.

THE SECOND NIGHT: The arguments against the view that personal identity consists in bodily identity are also suggested by Locke, as is the theory that memory is crucial. The argument that the memory theory is circular was made by Joseph Butler in "Of Personal Identity," an Appendix to his *Analogy of Religion,* first published in 1736. Locke's memory theory has been developed by a number of modern authors, including H.P. Grice, A.M. Quinton and, in a different direction, Sydney Shoemaker. The possibility of circumventing Butler's charge of circularity by an appeal to causation is noted by Shoemaker in his article "Persons and Their Pasts" (*American Philosophical Quarterly,* 1970) and by David Wiggins in *Identity and Spatial Temporal Continuity*. The "duplication argument" was apparently first used by the eighteenth-century freethinker, Antony Collins. Collins assumed that something like Locke's theory of personal identity was correct, and used the duplication argument to raise problems for the doctrine of immortality.

THE THIRD NIGHT: *Who is Julia?,* by Barbara Harris, is an engaging novel published in 1972. (Dr. Matthews had not yet thought of brain rejuvenations.)

Locke considers the possibility of the "consciousness" of a prince being transferred to the body of a cobbler. The idea of using the removal of a brain to suggest how this might happen comes from Sydney Shoemaker's seminal book, *Self-Knowledge and Self-Identity* (1963). In a number of important articles which are collected in his book *Problems of the Self* (1973), Bernard Williams has cleverly and articulately resisted the memory theory and the view that such a brain removal would amount to a body transplant. In particular, Williams has stressed the relevance of the duplication argument even in questions of terrestrial personal identity. Weirob's position in this essay is more inspired by Williams than anyone else. I have discussed Williams' arguments and related topics in "Can the Self Divide?" (*Journal of Philosophy*, 1972) and in a review of his book (*Journal of Philosophy*, 1976).

An important article on the themes which emerge toward the end of the dialogue is Derek Parfit's "Personal Identity" (*Philosophical Review*, 1971). This article, along with Locke's chapter and a number of other important chapters and articles by Hume, Shoemaker, Williams, and others are collected in my anthology *Personal Identity* (1975). A number of new articles on personal identity appear in Amelie Rorty (ed.), *The Identities of Persons* (1976), including my "The Importance of Being Identical" which addresses the questions raised by Cohen at the end.